Doodle Girl & Friends Presents:
open your Heart channel COLORING BOOK

Book One: Love

Diane Bleck

Copyright © 2015 Discovery Doodles, LLC
Illustrated by: Doodle Girl & Friends

All rights reserved.

ISBN: 151889707X
ISBN-13: 978-1518897078

www.doodleinstitute.com

THIS BOOK IS DEDICATED TO:

Doodle Girl & Friends

Contributors

Aeriana Blue
Aisha Wynter
Anke Lingertat
Ann Leach
April Banack
Ayla Tomasino
Beth Ytell Kang
Chariti Gent
Christine Bennett
Christine Li
Christine Summers
Claudia Ragsdale
Constance Wilson
Cynthia Lamontagne
Danielle Baird
Darlene Cothran
Denise Diggs
Diane Bleck
Doll Creelman
Dorie Wilson
Eleni Carey
Elizabeth White
Ellen Walan
Gracey Carey
Jessica Lewer
Joy Chan
Juliette Nelson
Kay Anderson
Leeanna Scott
Liliana Cruz
Linda Gillen
Linda Ragatz
Lisa Bice
Lisa Colpo
Lori Becker
Louma Sader
Luella Durand
Mary Ellen Maple
Melaine D'Cruze
Melinda Whitney
Michelle Bastian
Mike Schlegel
Nancy Marie Wiles
Natalia Gabrea
Patty D'Angelo
Peggy Robinson
PJ Deloatch
Rachel Cassondra
Ruthie Mason
Sara Ballard
Sarah Bratchell
Shauna Occhipinti
Sheryl May
Sophia Carey
Stephanie Carey
Tammy Judd Jenny
Tanina Messina
Therese Prentice
Tracey Joseph
Tracy Bedford
Tracy McQueen
Vicky Hemming
Wendy Palmer

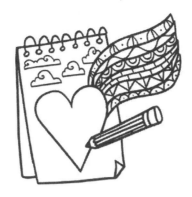

"When you put pen to paper you open your heart channel for ideas, insights and inspirations."

Diane Bleck is The Doodle Girl, and she is on a mission to change the world by inspiring people to discover, dream and doodle at home, school and work. She has spent her career bringing doodling to businesses, healthcare communities, education programs and families. The Doodle Institute opened in 2014 to teach others how putting pen to paper opens your heart channel and lets you access ideas, insights, and inspiration.

When Diane began to share her passion and mini-lessons on Periscope (@discoverydoodles), she cultivated wonderful enthusiasm in a diverse community that eventually led to the formation of the 'Doodle Girl & Friends' Facebook group. It's a magical place were the sharing of doodles and loving encouragement fills the space without fears of judgment.

It's been called the most creative place on the internet and has been truly transformational as many are finding the courage to share their doodles at any stage in their creative journey. For the members of the group, their Facebook feeds have become a stream of awesome doodles and creativity.

A seed was planted by the recent launch of *The Doodle Coloring Book* by Danielle Baird, a dear friend of Diane. Inspired by all the wonderful creativity and joy that has been sparked by this coloring book, an idea began to grow to create a collaborative coloring book!

And so it was decided, the Doodle Girl & Friends would publish a coloring book, and the pages would be created by the members of the Facebook group. Doodles poured in, each one inspiring others to join in. The love and encouragement of fellow doodle friends of every skill level was so amazing!

It was unanimously decided the first book in the series should be titled 'LOVE.'

This coloring book was created by The Doodle Girl & Friends to share our love with you and help you open your heart and unlock creativity. So, we invite you to dive in, get messy, start coloring and be part of the magic! Don't let fear stand in your way; color any self-doubt away, and let your dreams shine through. We hope this coloring book will help you take time to connect pen to paper, and in doing so, rediscover your creative spirit. We want this to be a coloring book for all ages, because our love connects us at any stage in life.

We invite you to share your creations online and use the hashtag #DGFBook1 so we can find you and celebrate your creative spirit. We also encourage you to join us on Facebook. Find the link to the Doodle Girl & Friends at: www.doodleinstitute.com

Made with love. Happy coloring!

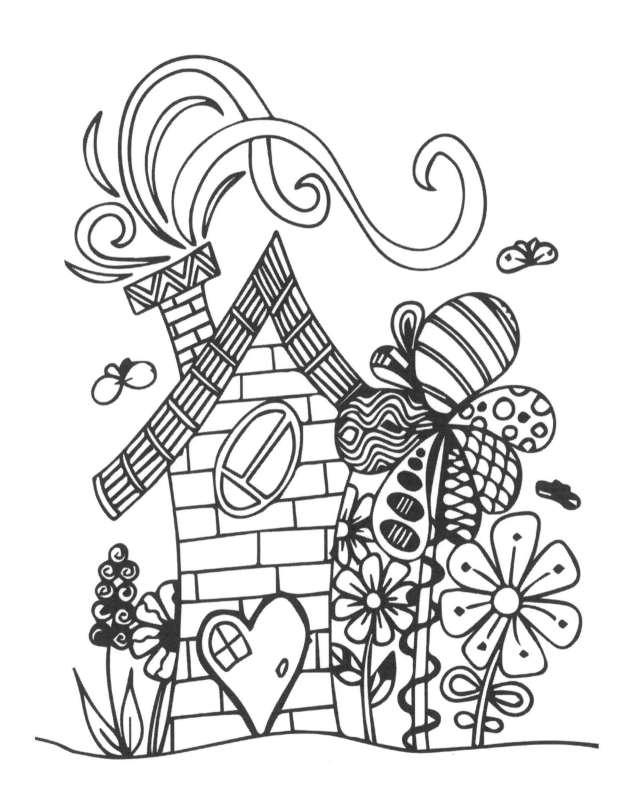

ILLUSTRATED BY: CYNTHIA LAMONTAGNE		COLORED BY:

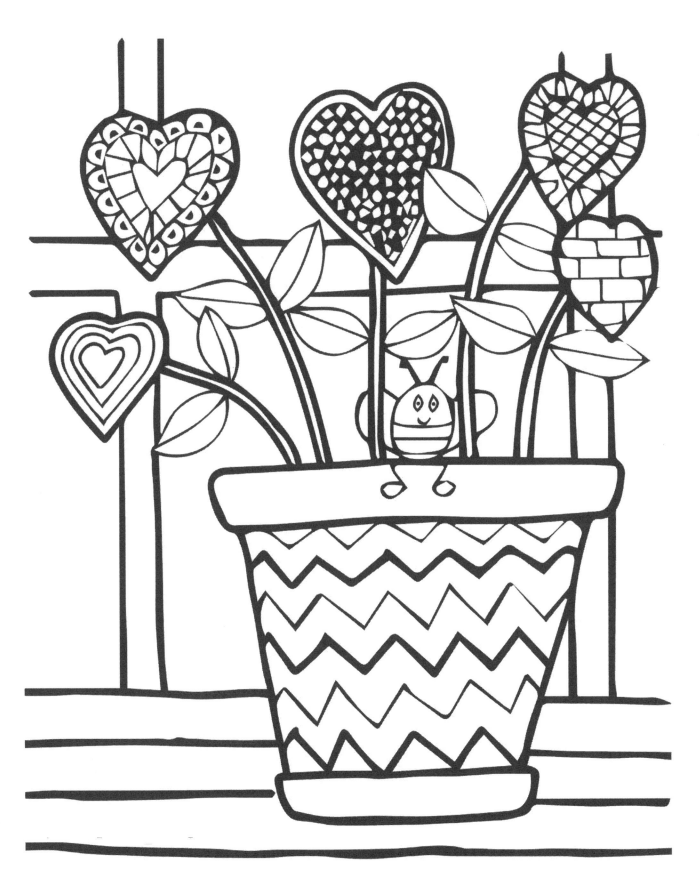

ILLUSTRATED BY: CLAUDIA RAGSDALECOLORED BY:

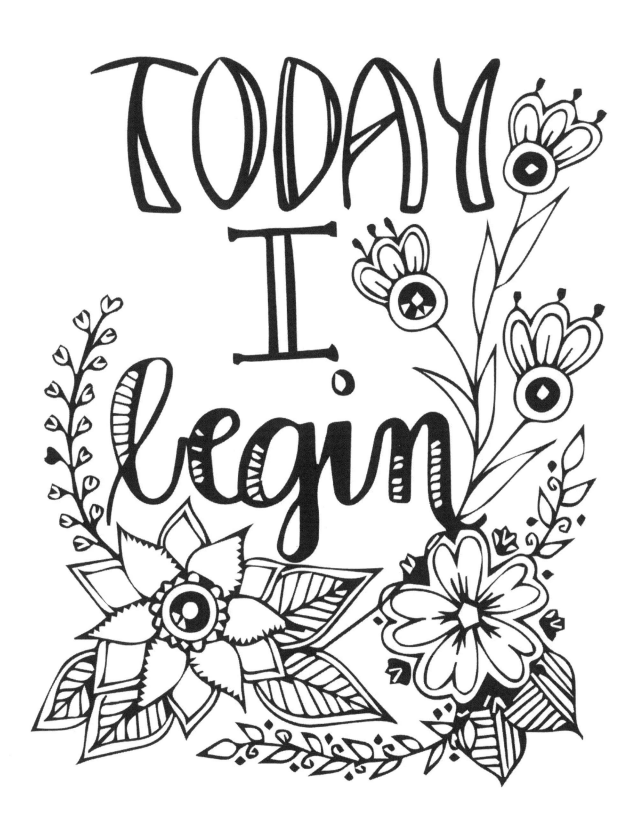

ILLUSTRATED BY: LISA BICE

COLORED BY:

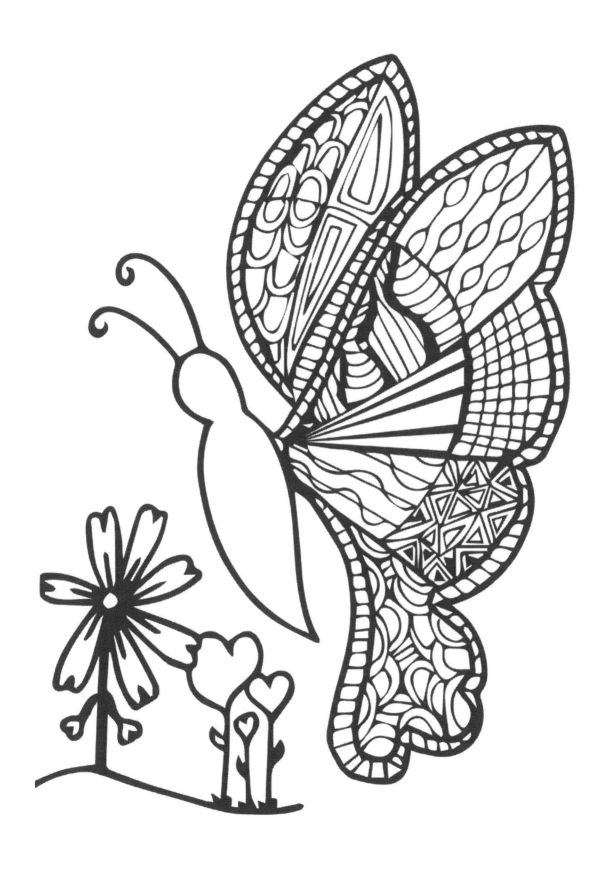

ILLUSTRATED BY: DARLENE COTHRAN				COLORED BY:

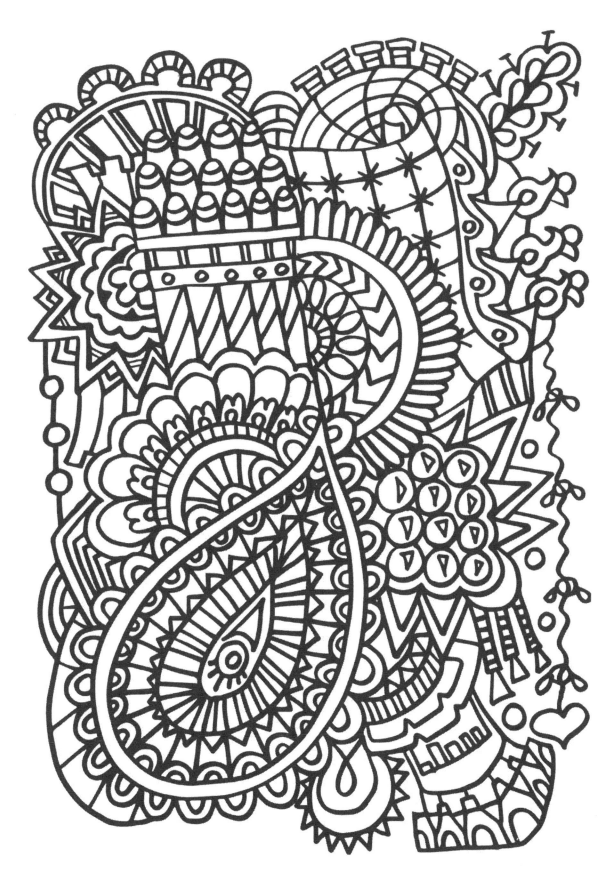

ILLUSTRATED BY: CHRISTINE BENNETT COLORED BY:

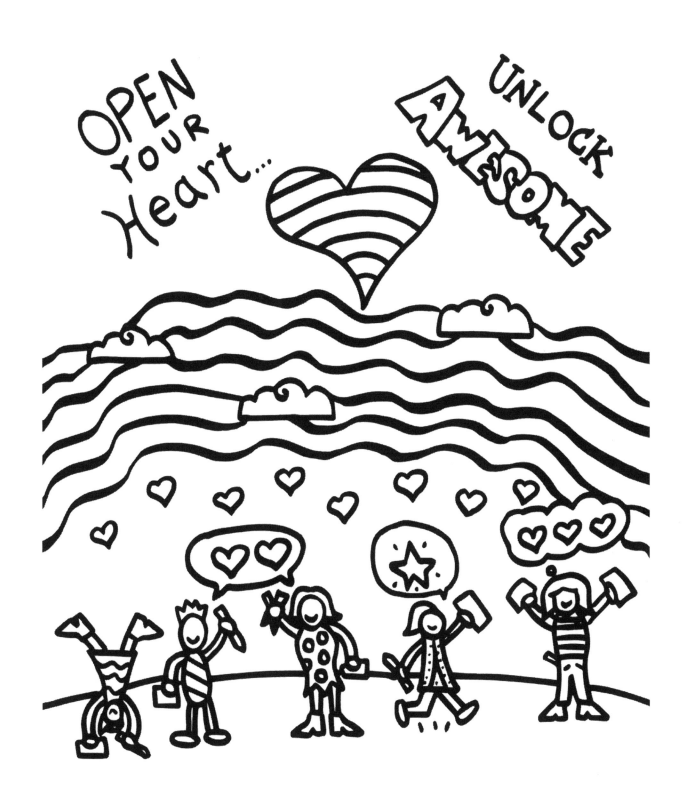

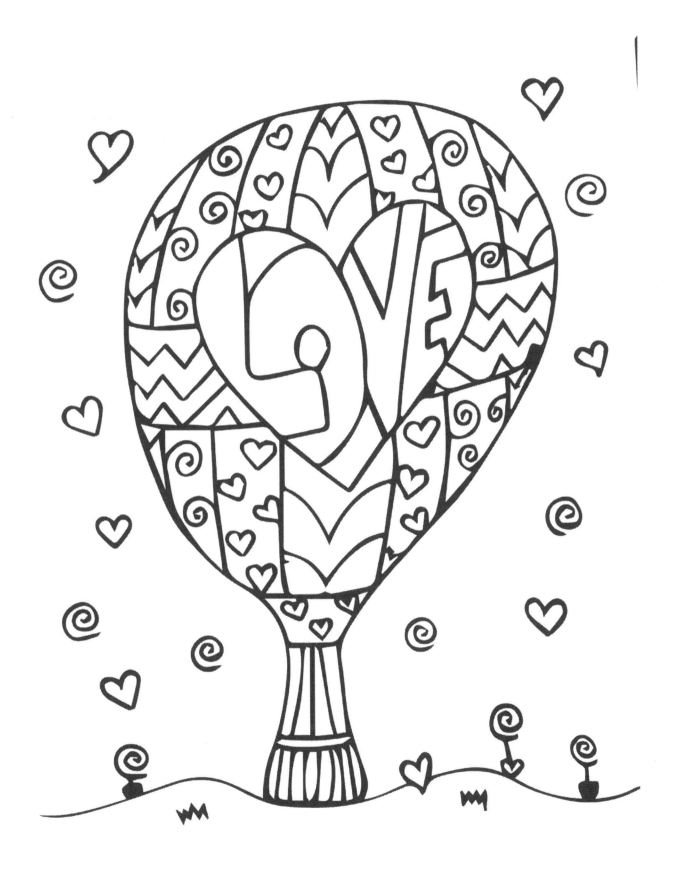

ILLUSTRATED BY: WENDY PALMER   COLORED BY:

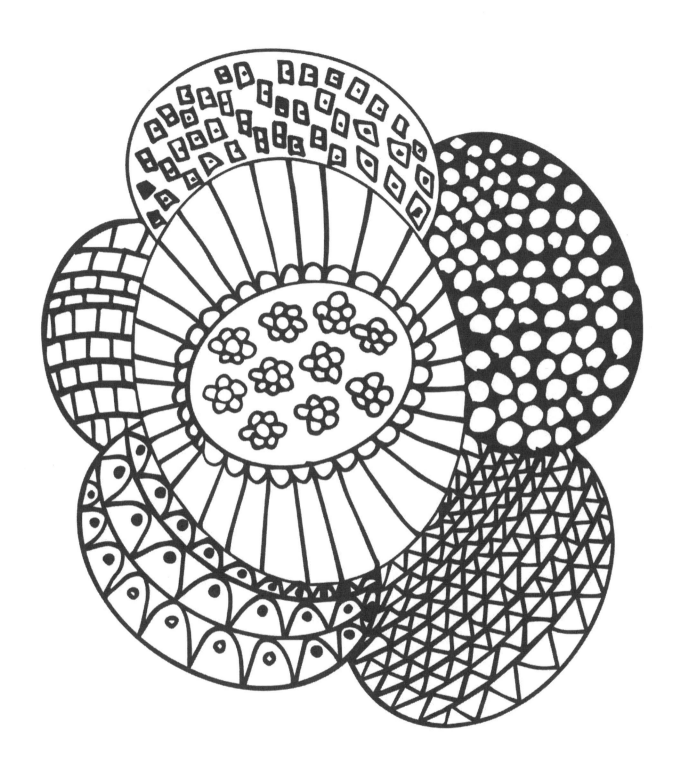

ILLUSTRATED BY: CHRISTINE SUMMERS   COLORED BY:

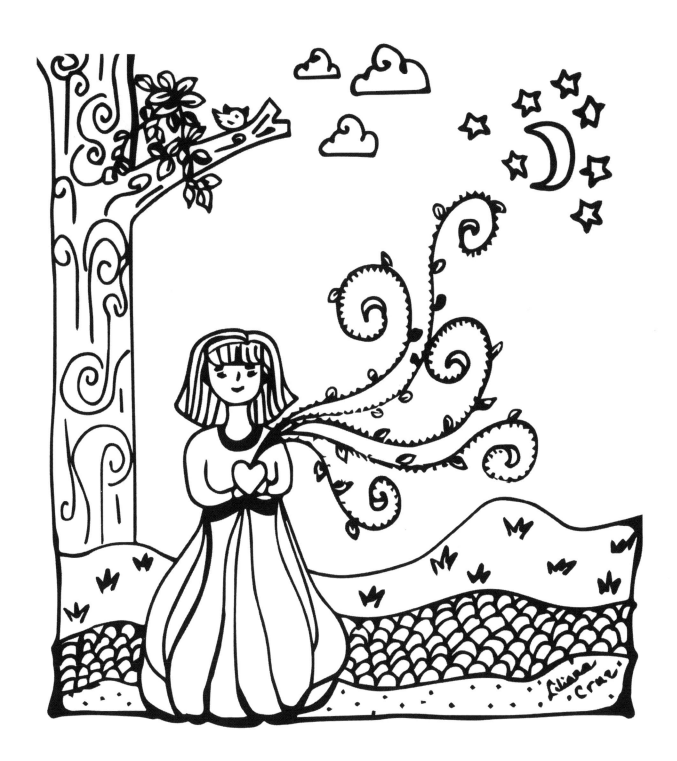

ILLUSTRATED BY: LILLIANA CRUZ		COLORED BY:

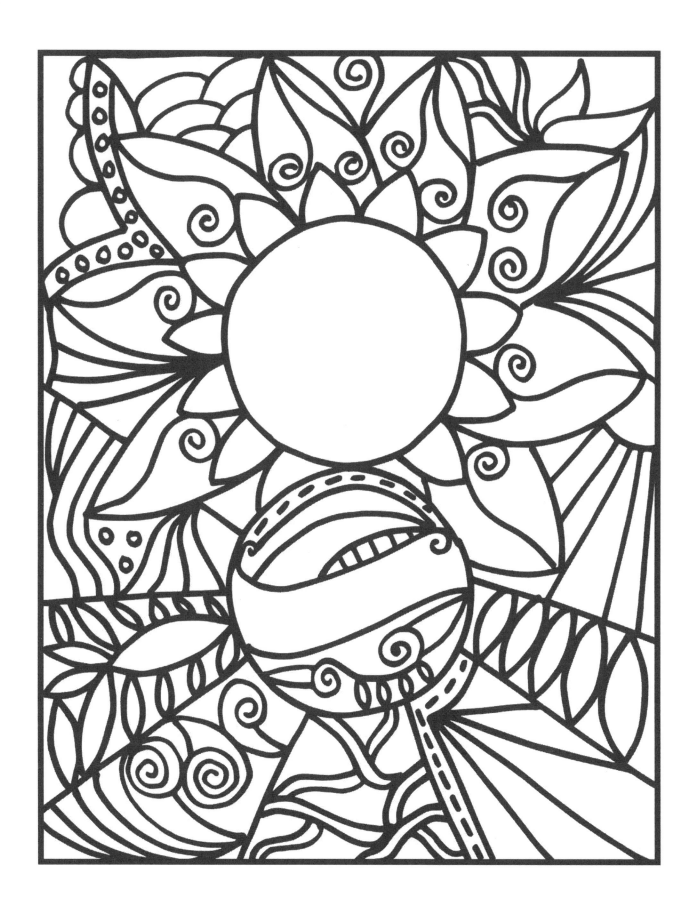

ILLUSTRATED BY: AERIANA BLUE   COLORED BY:

LLUSTRATED BY: RACHEL CASSONDRA   COLORED BY:

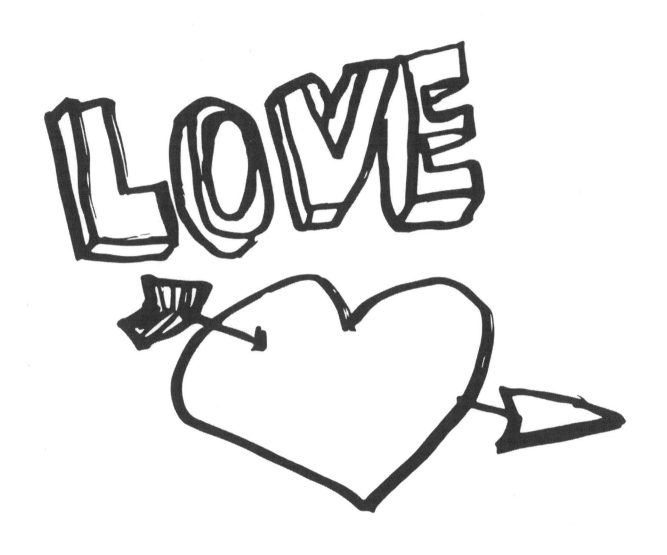

ILLUSTRATED BY: LISA COLPO					COLORED BY:

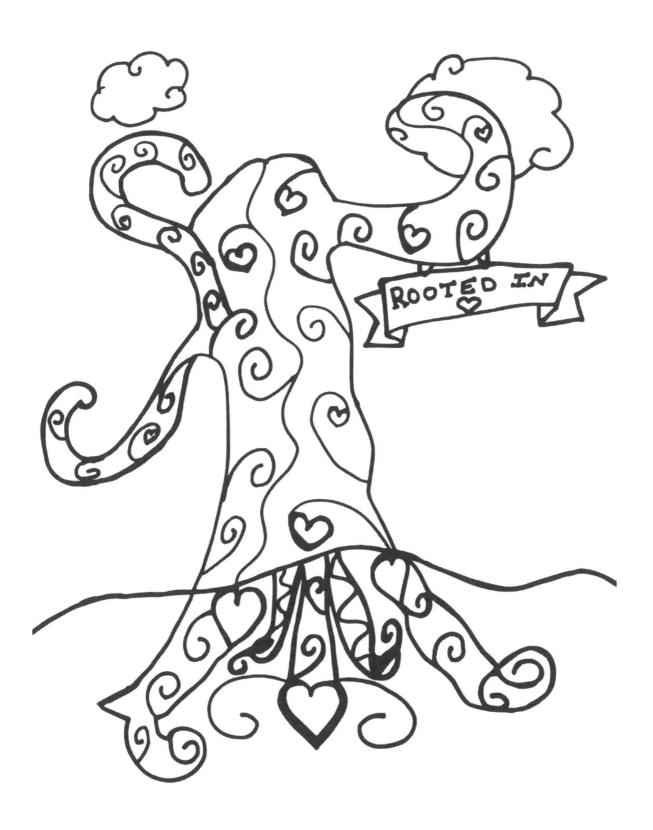

ILLUSTRATED BY: SHAUNA OCCHIPINTI					COLORED BY:

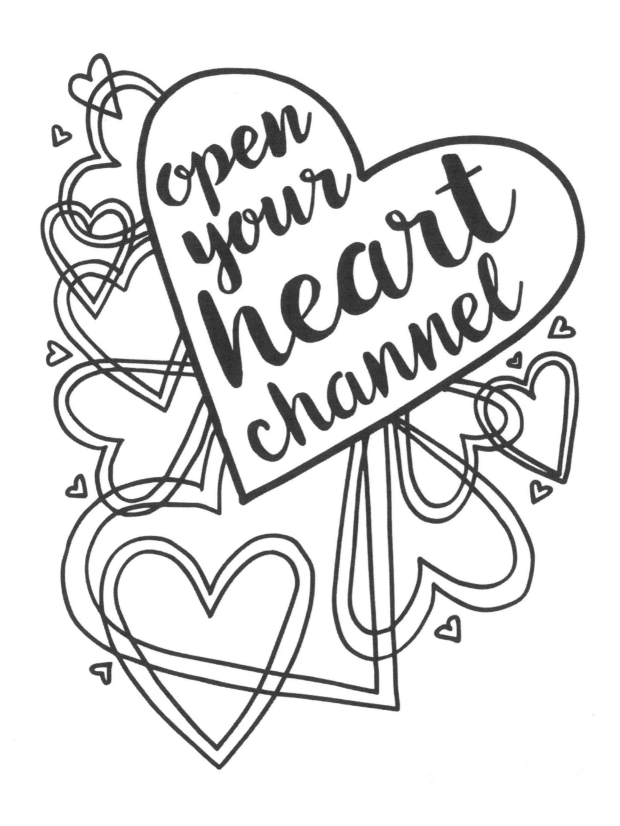

ILLUSTRATED BY: DANIELLE BAIRD   COLORED BY:

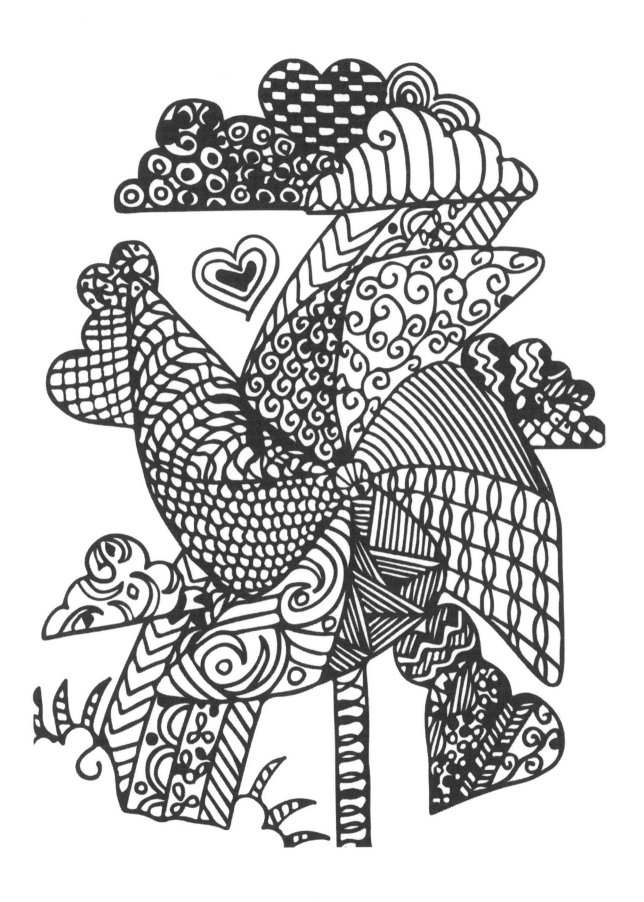

ILLUSTRATED BY: SHERYL MAY   COLORED BY:

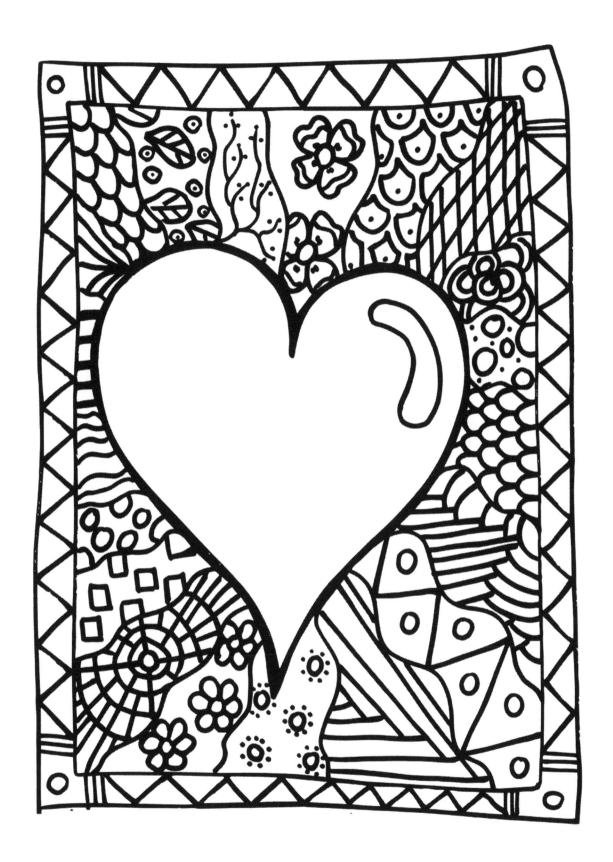

ILLUSTRATED BY: ANKE LINGERTAT					COLORED BY:

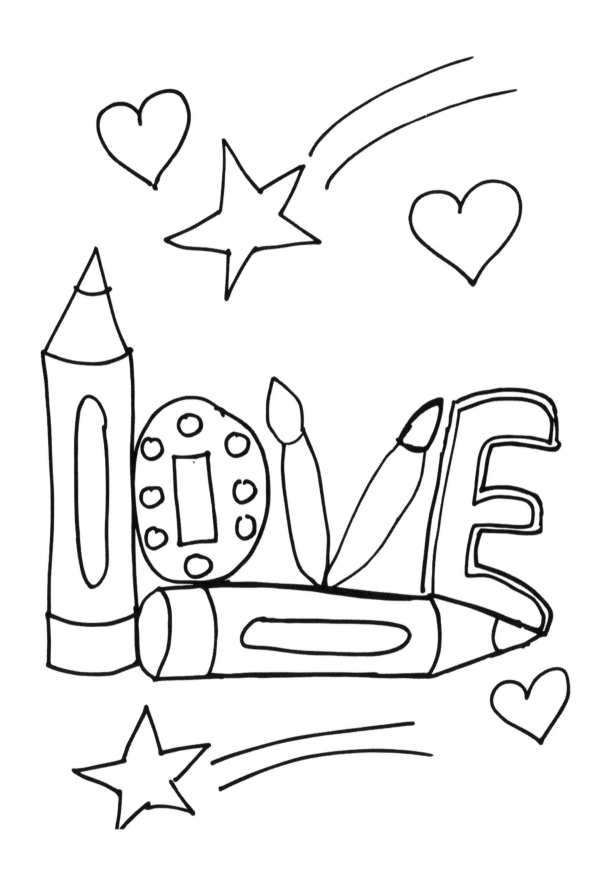

ILLUSTRATED BY: TRACEY JOSEPH   COLORED BY:

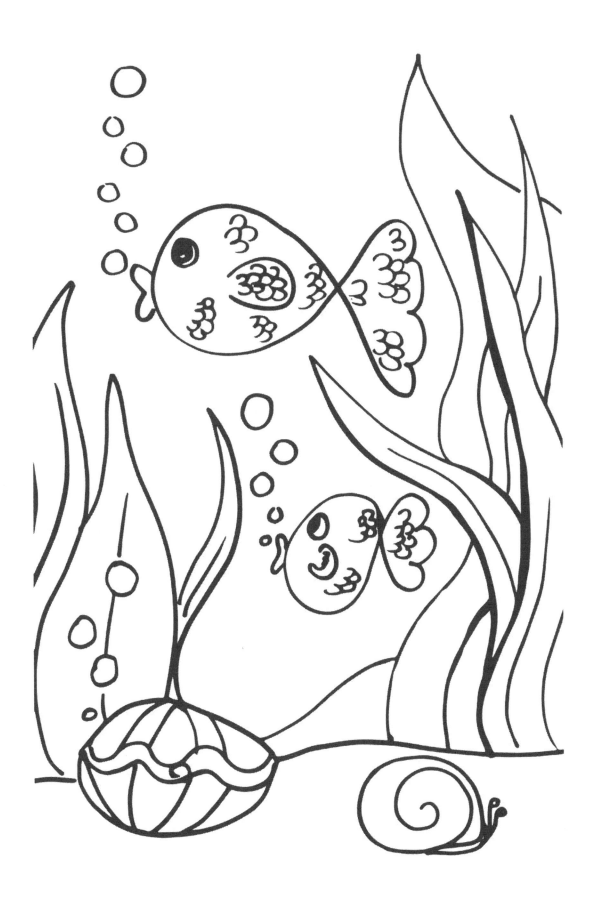

ILLUSTRATED BY: NANCY MARIE WILES   COLORED BY:

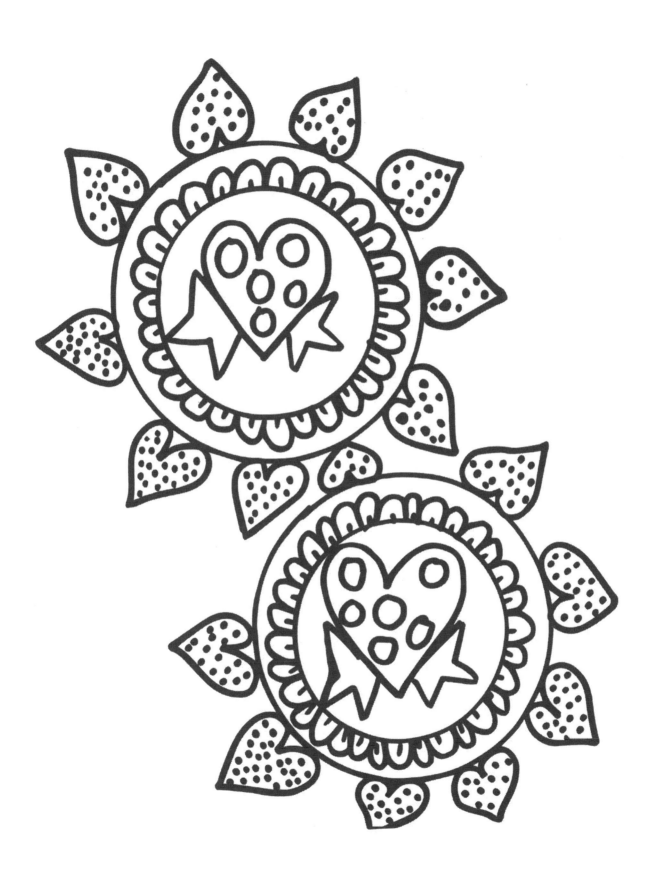

ILLUSTRATED BY: ELENI CAREY   COLORED BY:

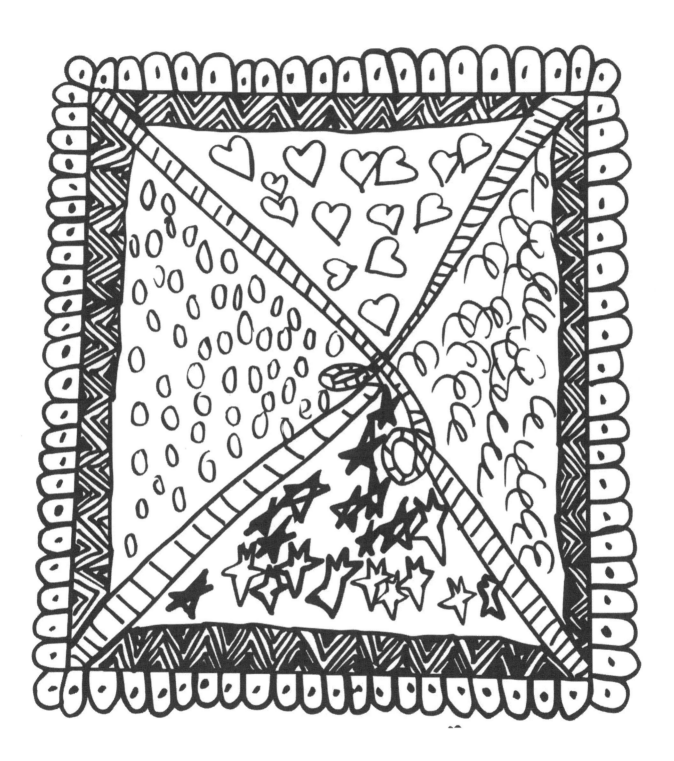

ILLUSTRATED BY: SOPHIA CAREY   COLORED BY:

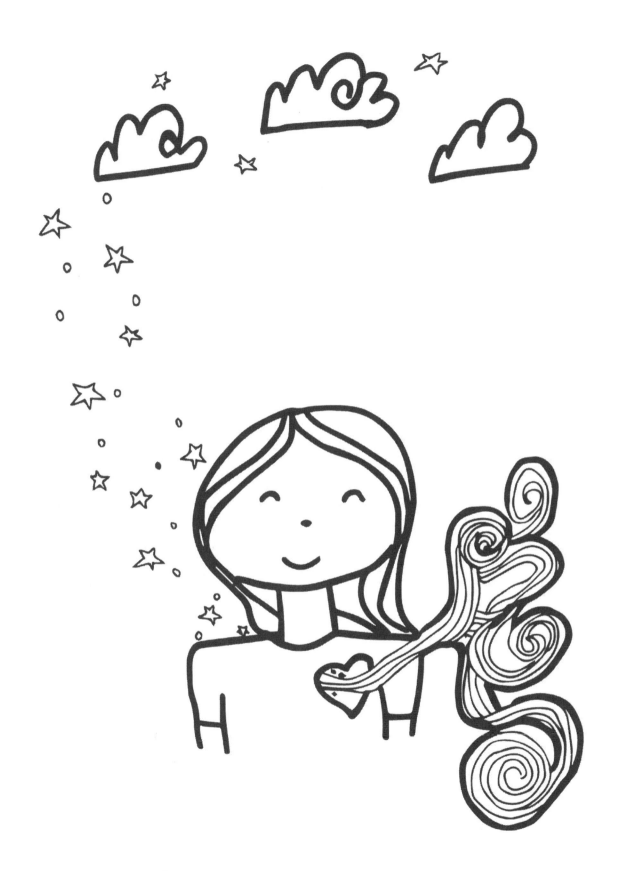

ILLUSTRATED BY: GRACE CAREY   COLORED BY:

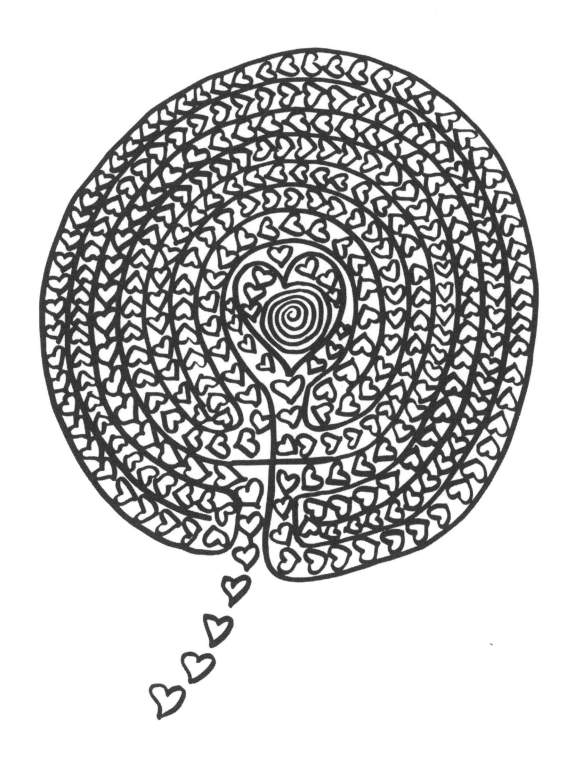

ILLUSTRATED BY: SARA BALLARD   COLORED BY:

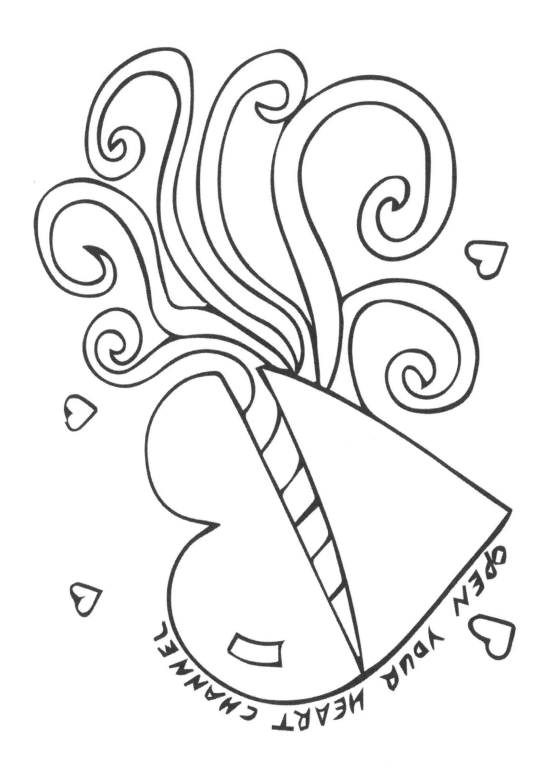

ILLUSTRATED BY: TRACY BEDFORD   COLORED BY:

ILLUSTRATED BY: PJ DELOATCH   COLORED BY:

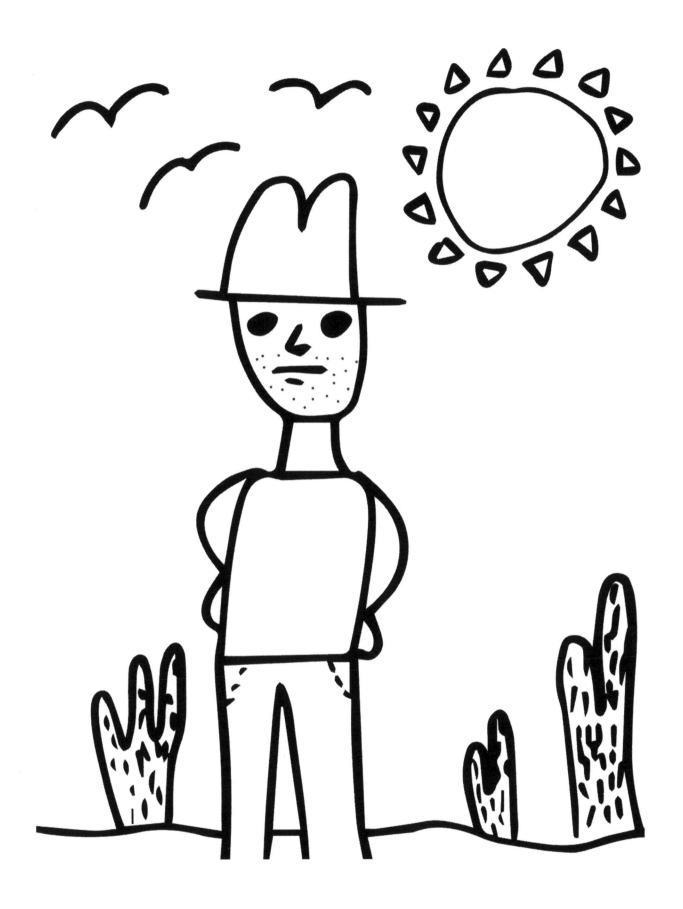

ILLUSTRATED BY: AYLA TOMASINO   COLORED BY:

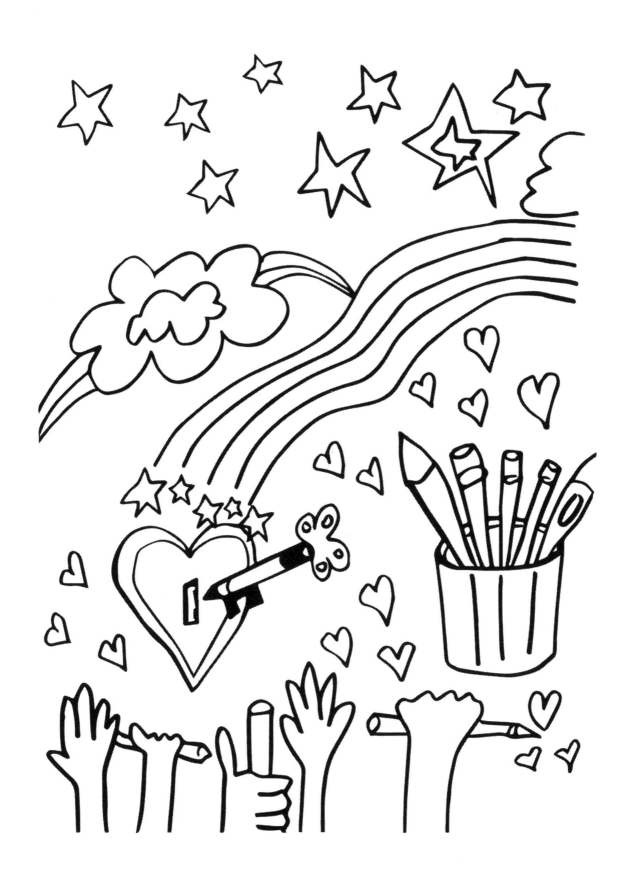

ILLUSTRATED BY: TAMMY JUDD JENNY				COLORED BY:

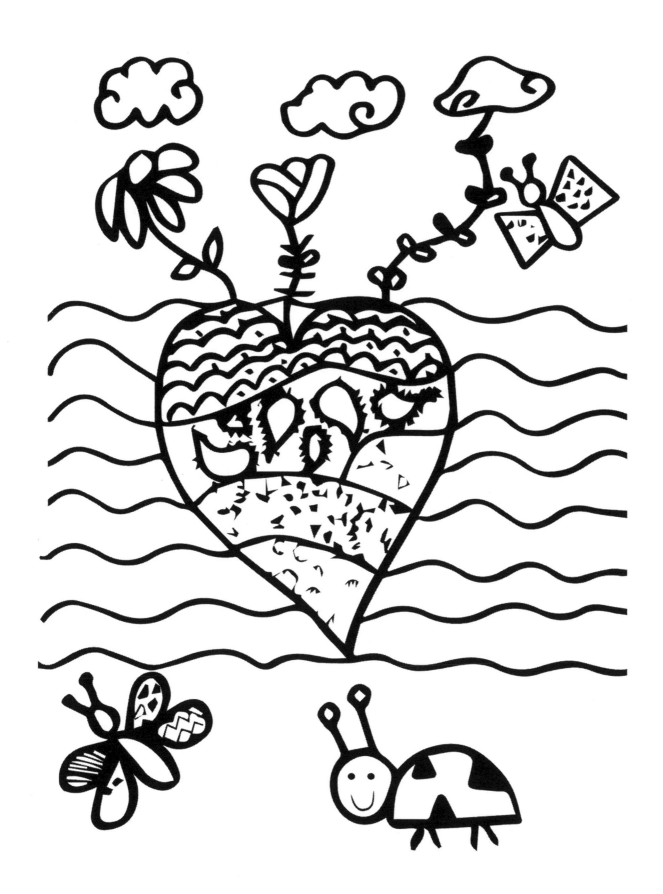

ILLUSTRATED BY: ELLEN WALAN   COLORED BY:

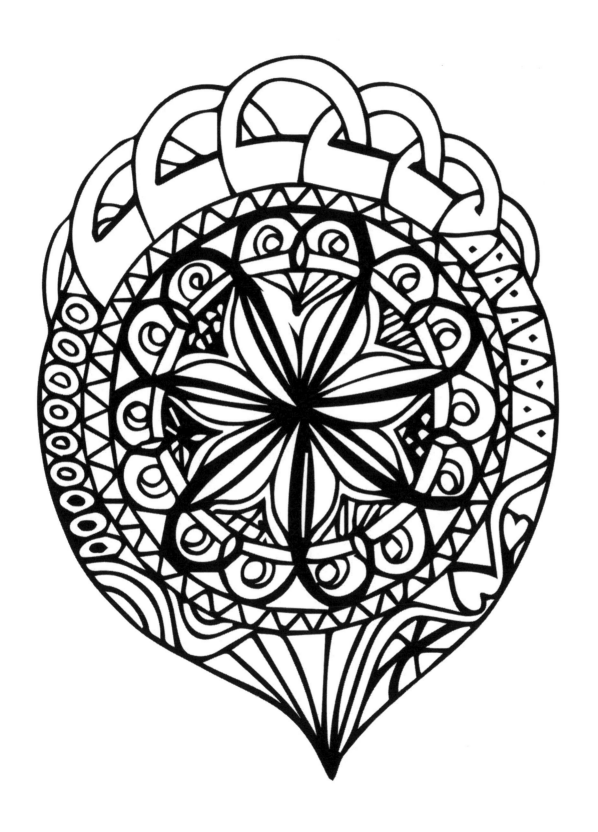

ILLUSTRATED BY: LINDA GILLEN   COLORED BY:

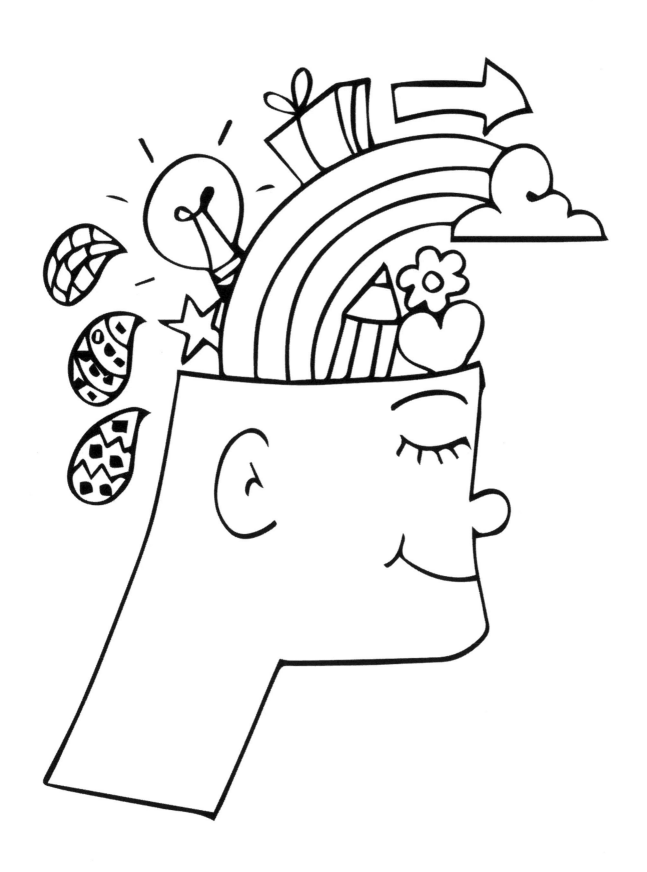

ILLUSTRATED BY: MELAINE D'CRUZE   COLORED BY:

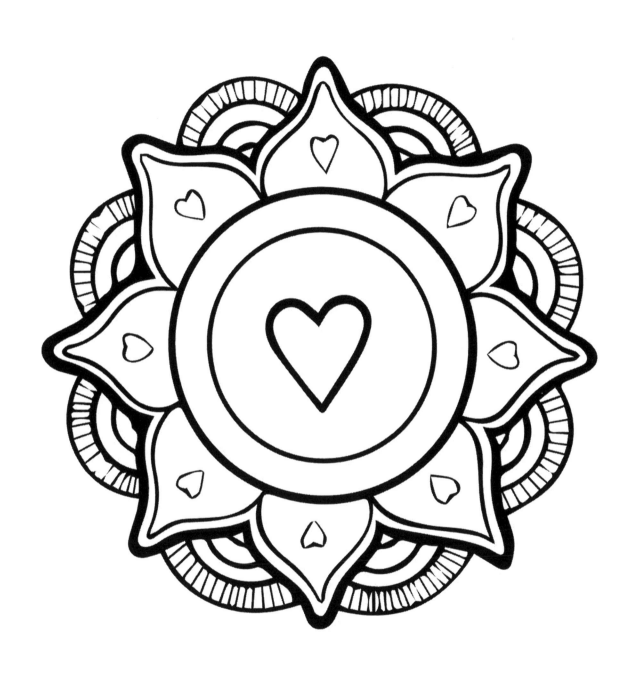

ILLUSTRATED BY: VICKY HEMMING   COLORED BY:

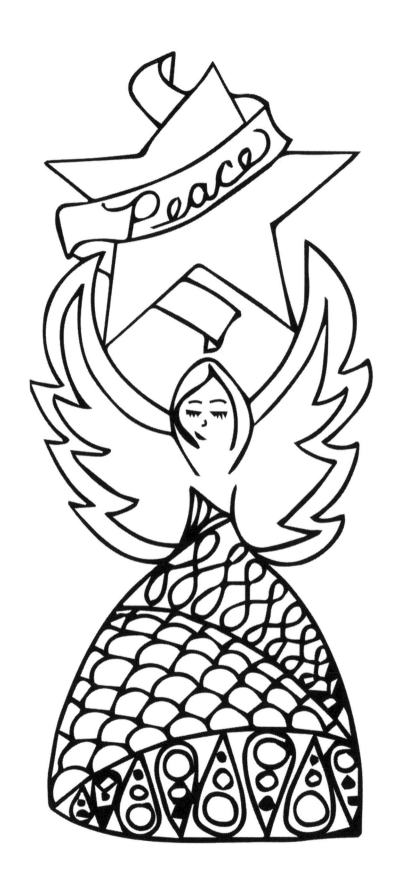

ILLUSTRATED BY: LEEANNA SCOTT   COLORED BY:

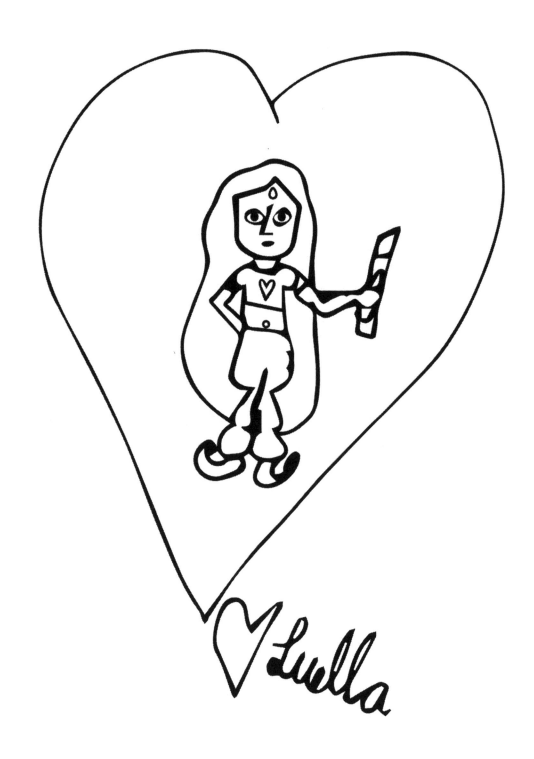

ILLUSTRATED BY: LUELLA DURAND   COLORED BY

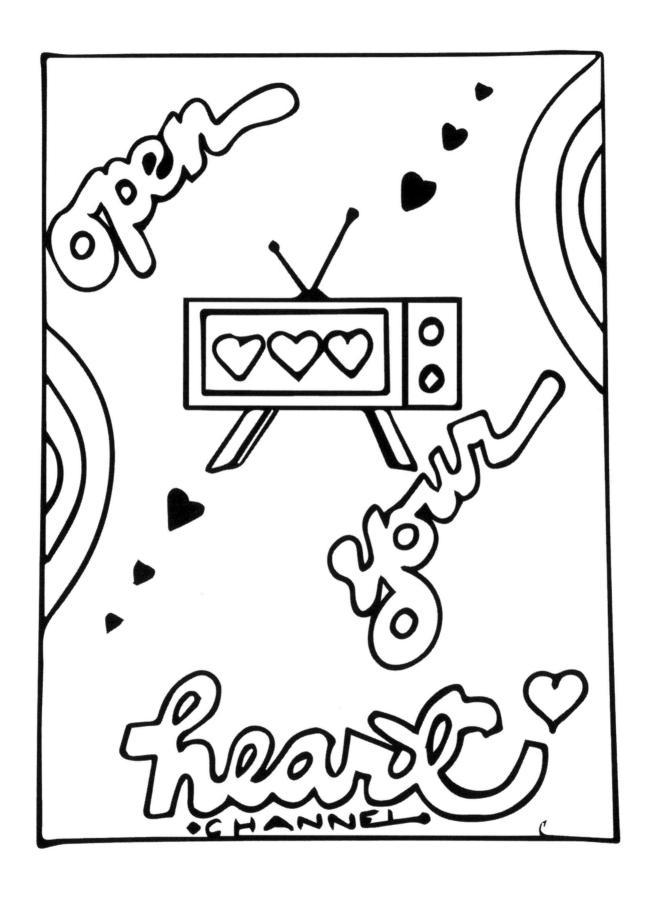

ILLUSTRATED BY: CHARITI GENT		COLORED BY:

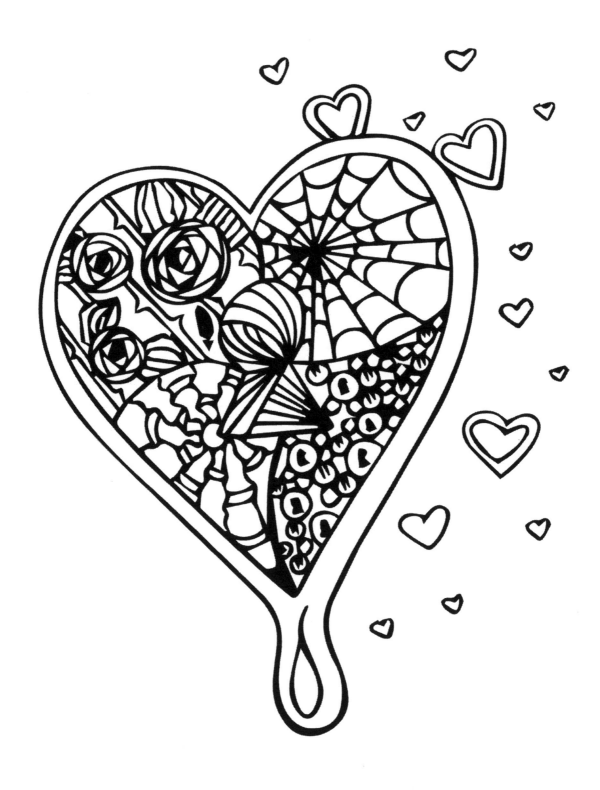

ILLUSTRATED BY: CONSTANCE WILSON   COLORED BY:

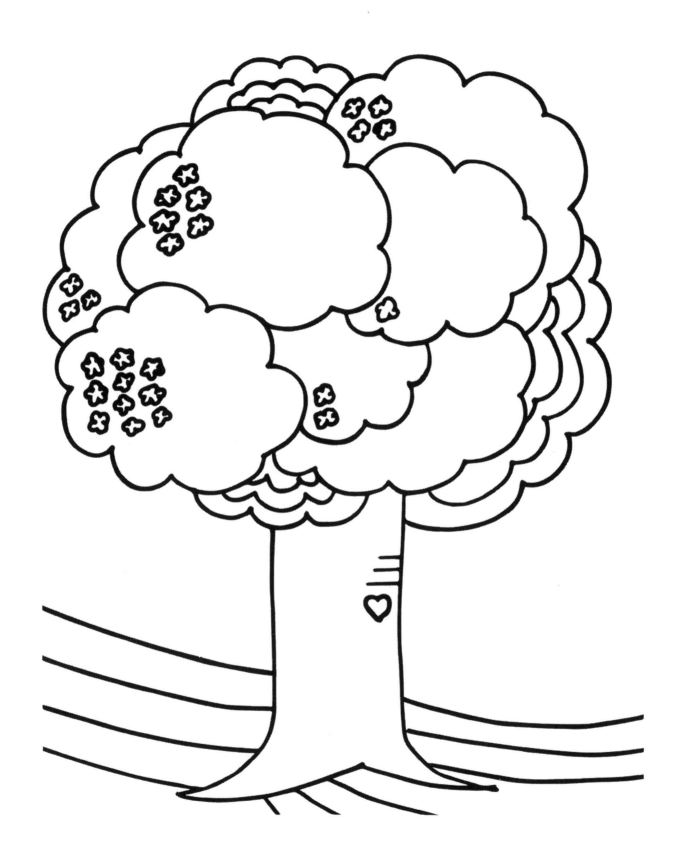

ILLUSTRATED BY: ELIZABETH WHITE   COLORED BY:

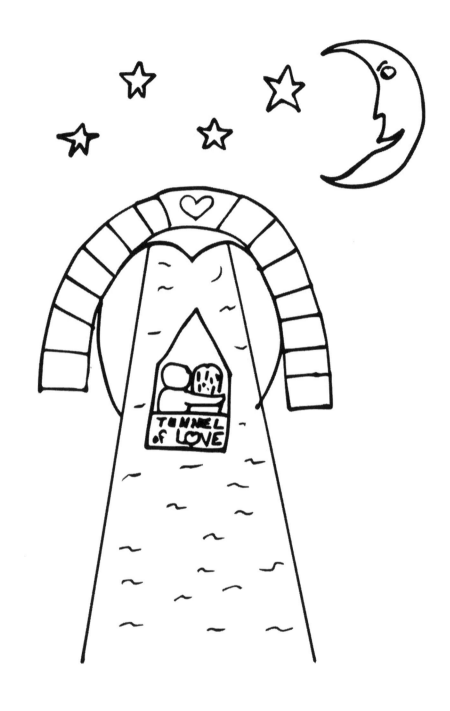

ILLUSTRATED BY: MARY ELLEN MAPLE   COLORED BY:

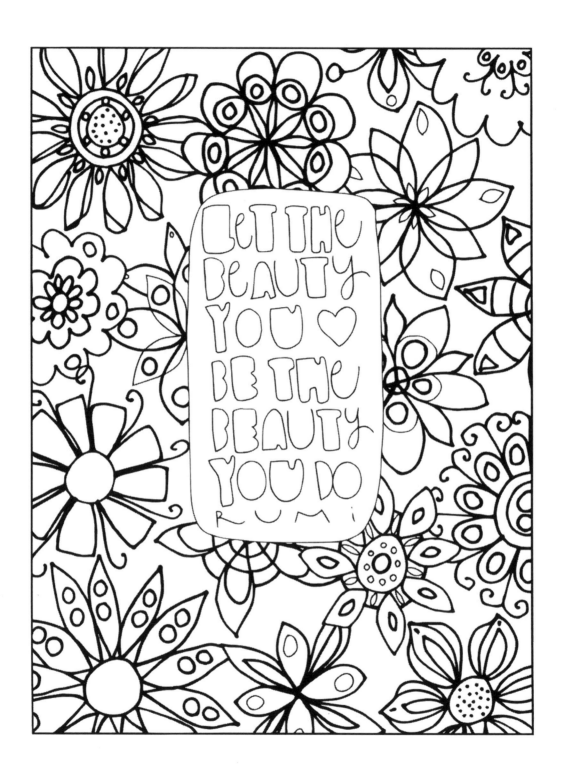

ILLUSTRATED BY: JULIETTE NELSON COLORED BY:

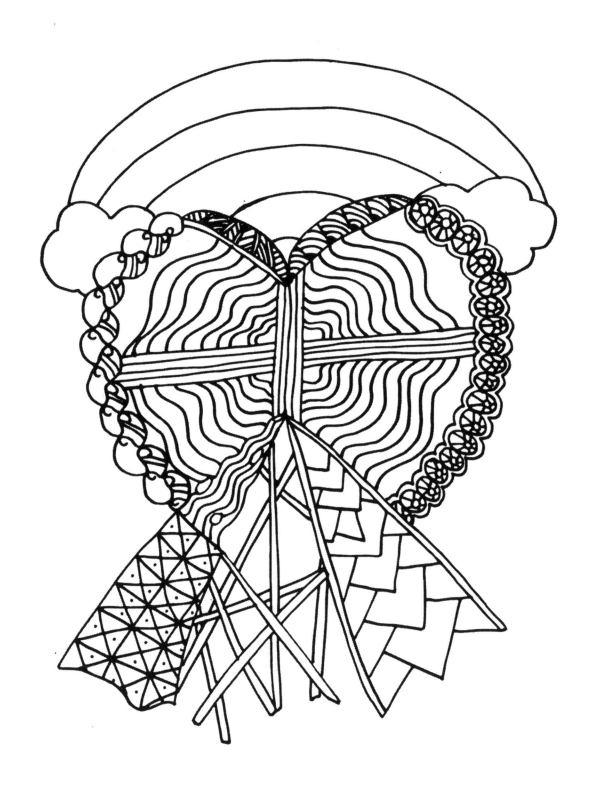

ILLUSTRATED BY: JOY CHAN   COLORED BY:

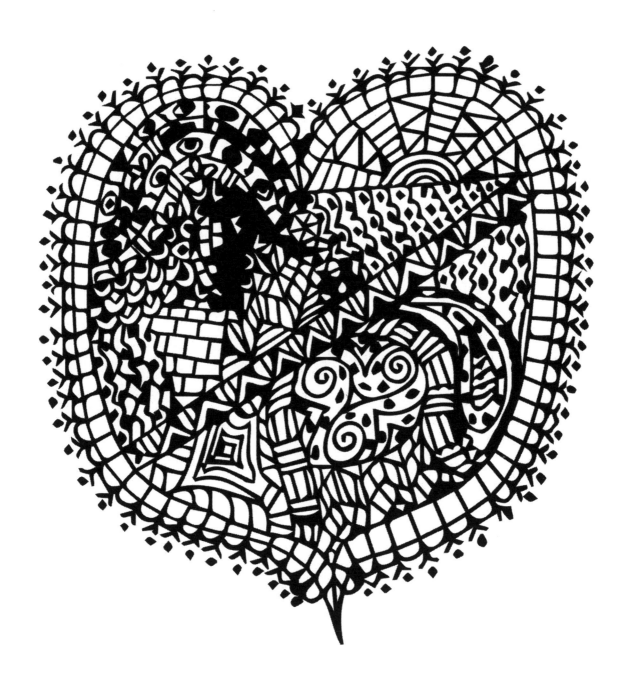

ILLUSTRATED BY: PATTY D'ANGELO

COLORED BY:

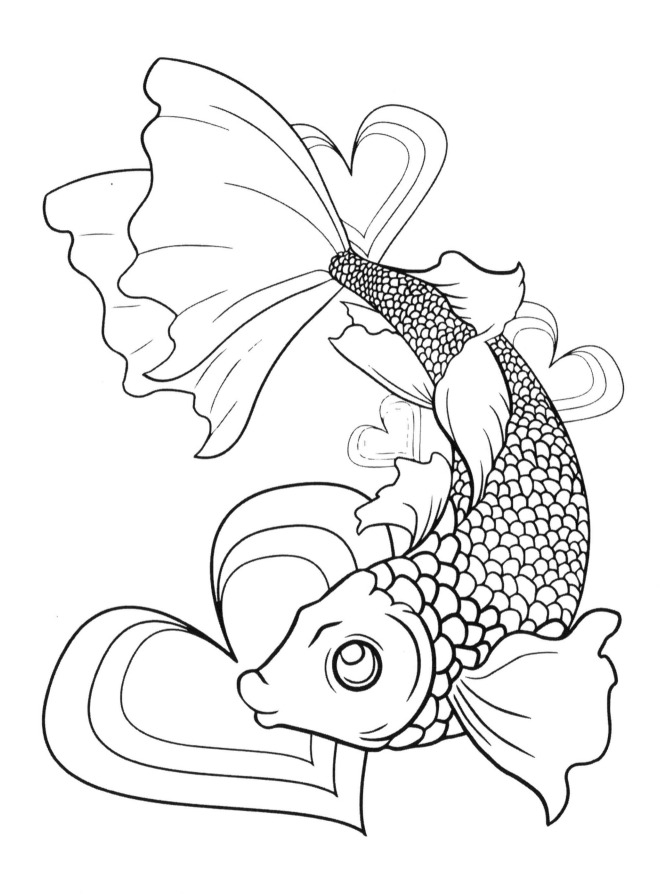

ILLUSTRATED BY: TRACY MCQUEEN   COLORED BY:

ILLUSTRATED BY: APRIL BANACK

COLORED BY:

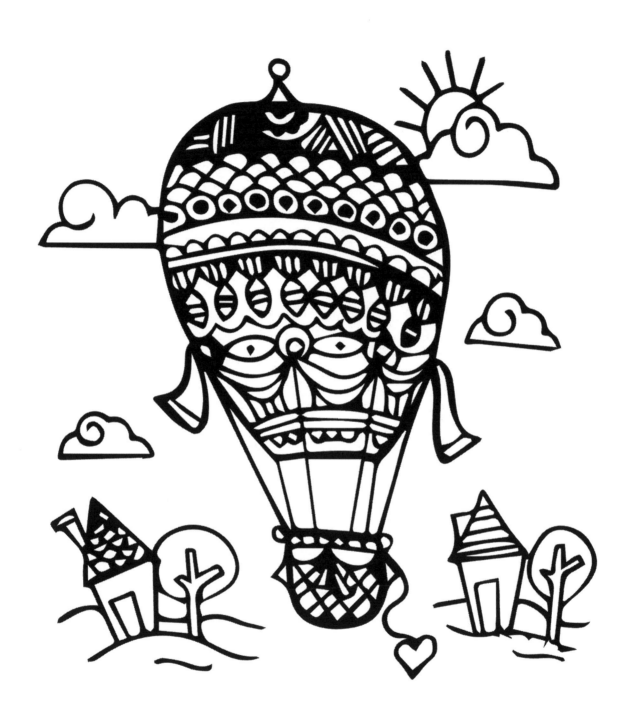

ILLUSTRATED BY: PEGGY ROBINSON					COLORED BY:

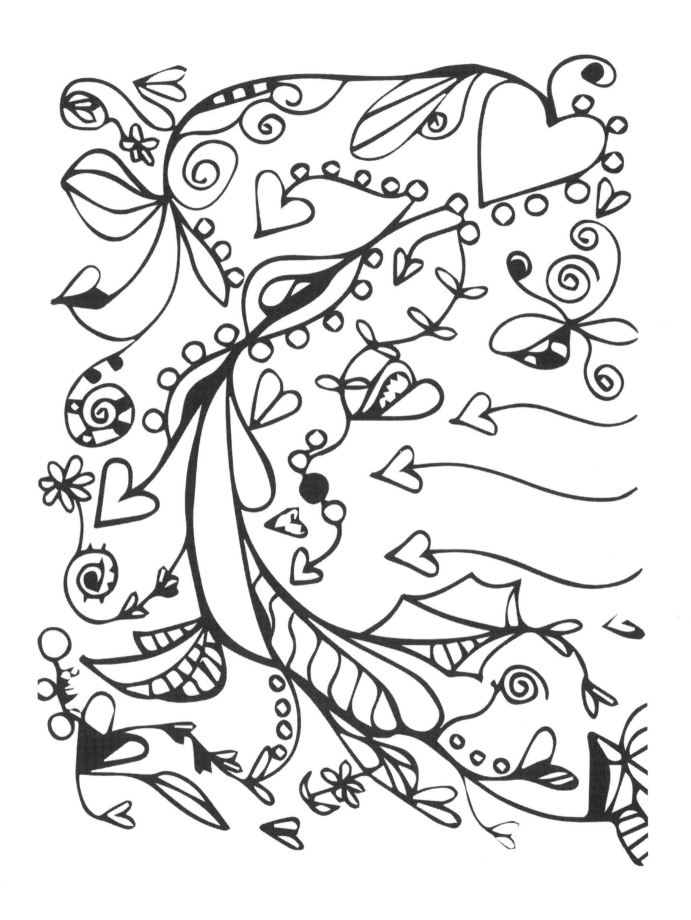

ILLUSTRATED BY: BETH YTELL KANG   COLORED BY:

ILLUSTRATED BY: TANINA MESSINA   COLORED BY:

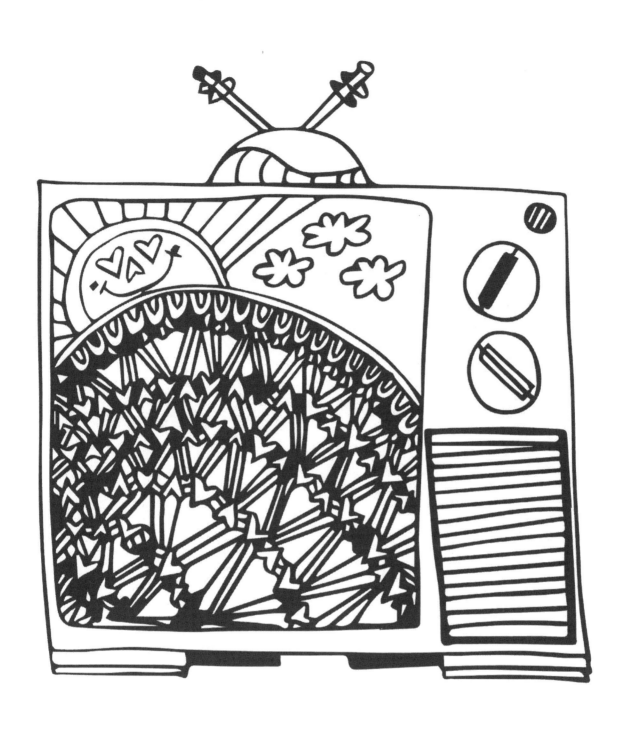

ILLUSTRATED BY: MELINDA WHITNEY   COLORED BY:

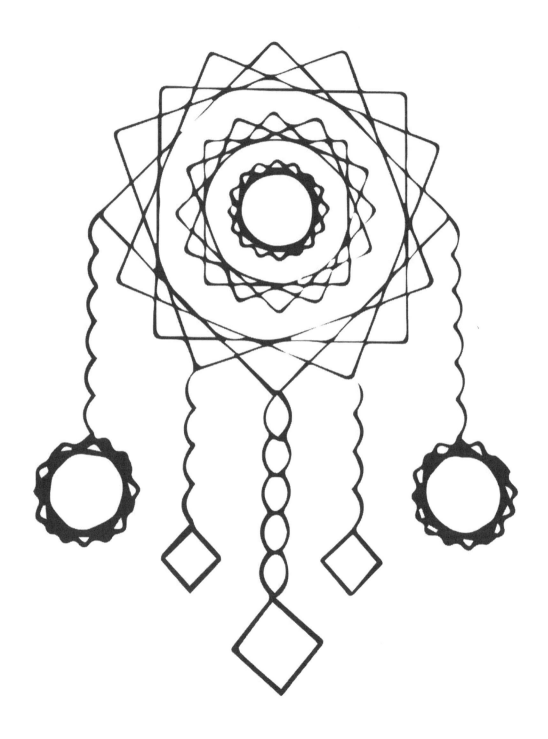

ILLUSTRATED BY: DORIE WILSON   COLORED BY:

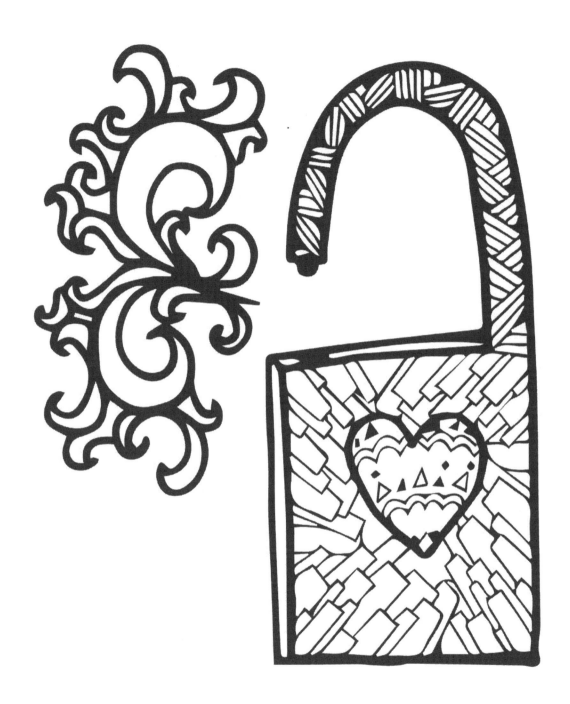

I

LLUSTRATED BY: STEPHANIE CAREY   COLORED BY:

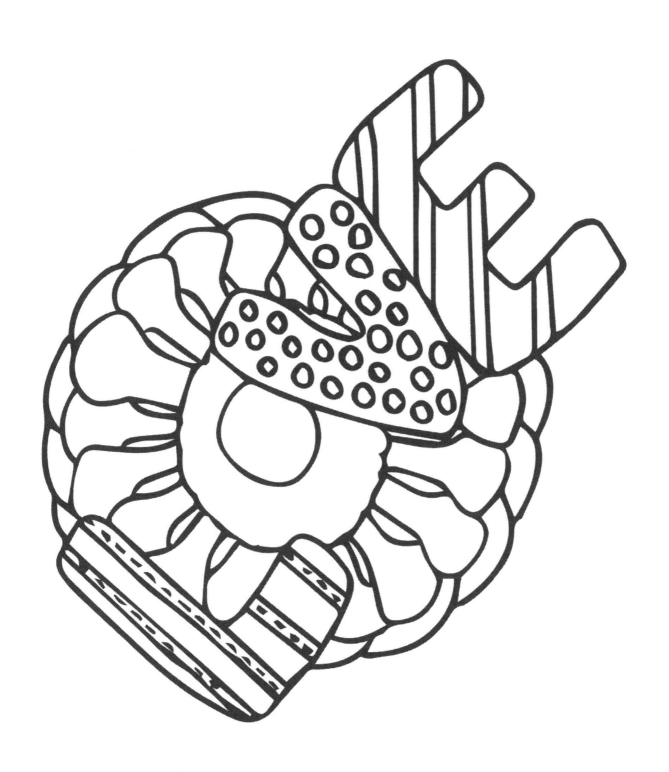

ILLUSTRATED BY: LORI BECKER   COLORED BY:

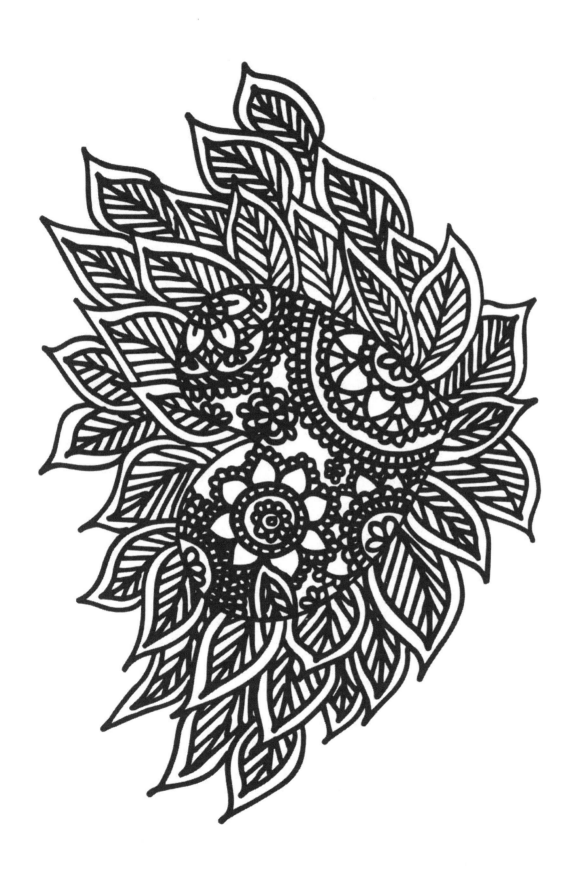

ILLUSTRATED BY: LOUMA SADER COLORED BY:

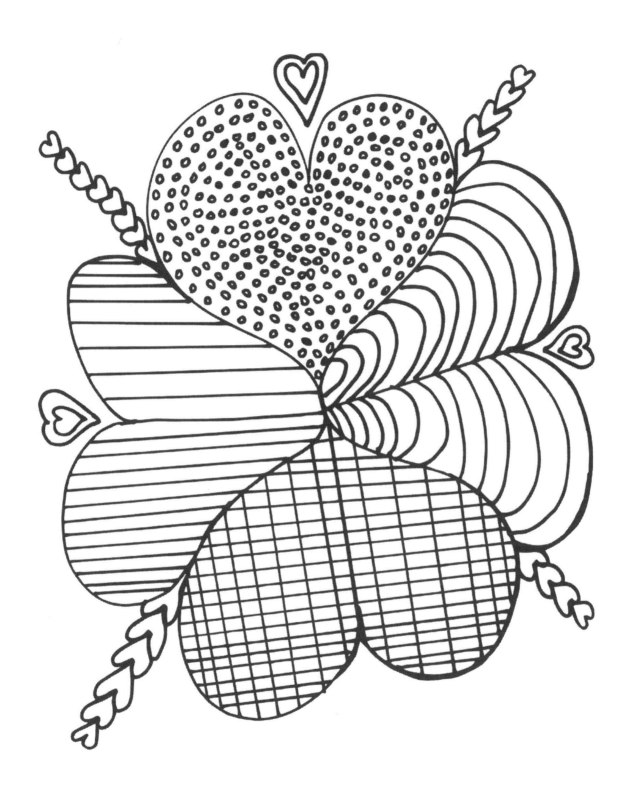

ILLUSTRATED BY: THERESE PRENTICE   COLORED BY:

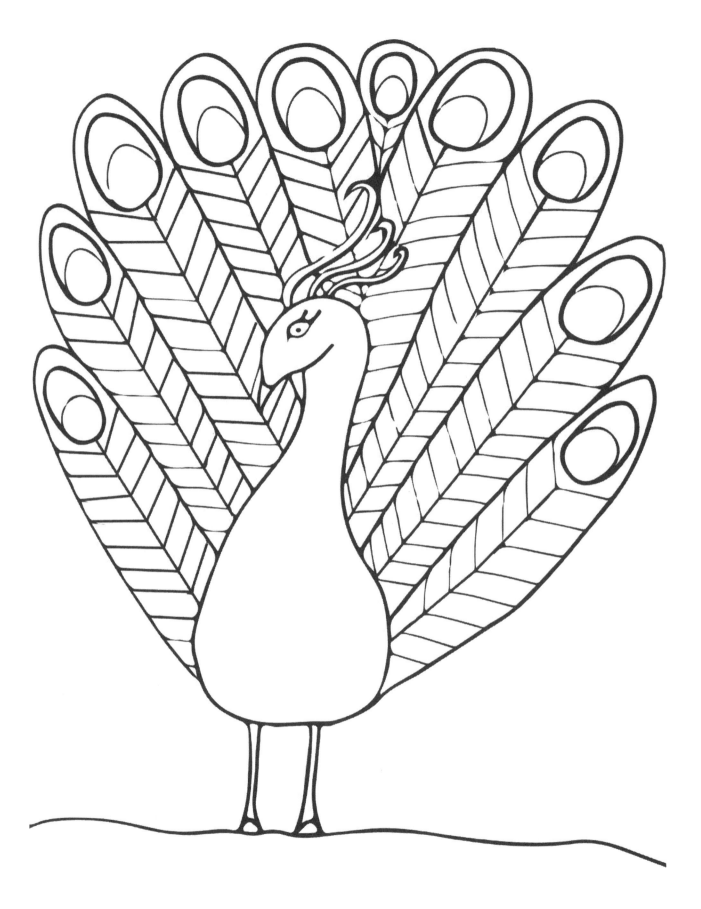

ILLUSTRATED BY: AISHA WYNTER   COLORED BY:

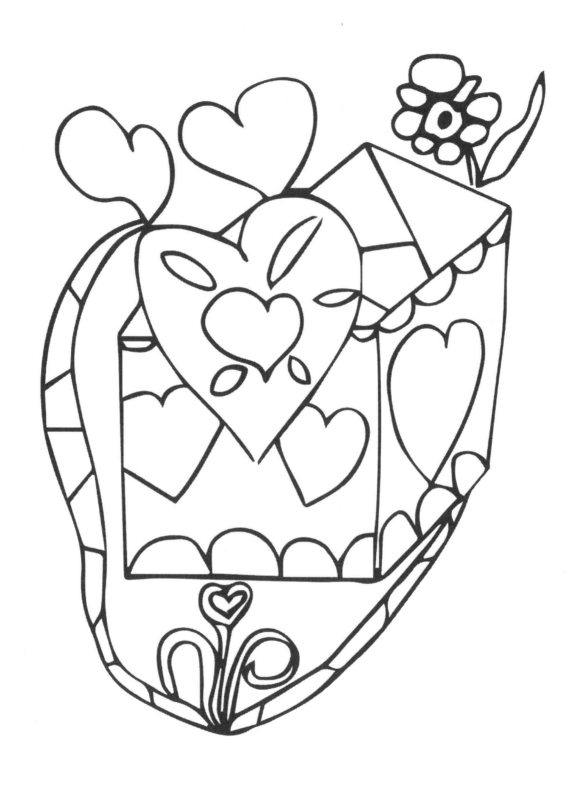

ILLUSTRATED BY: DOLL CREELMAN   COLORED BY:

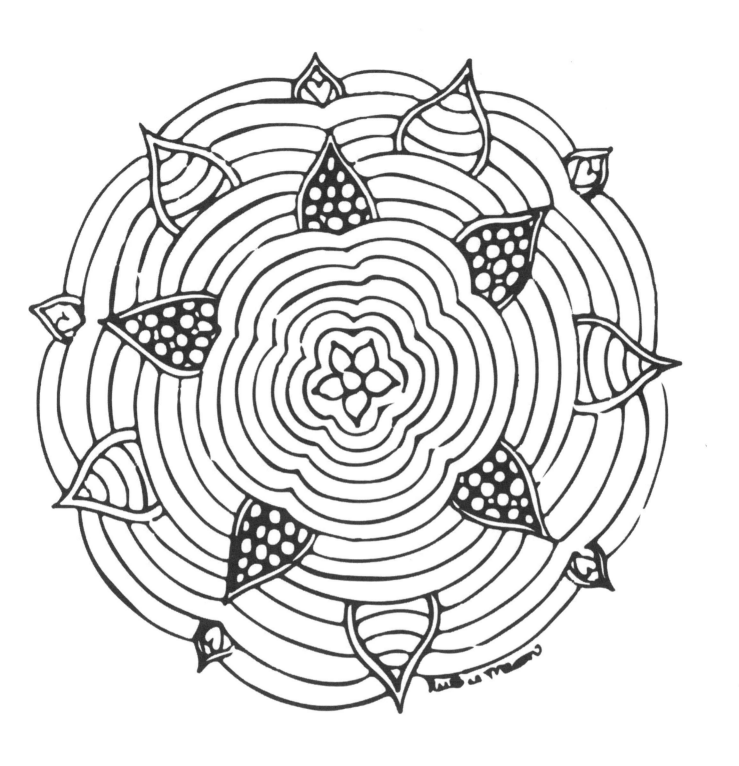

ILLUSTRATED BY: RUTHIE MASON   COLORED BY:

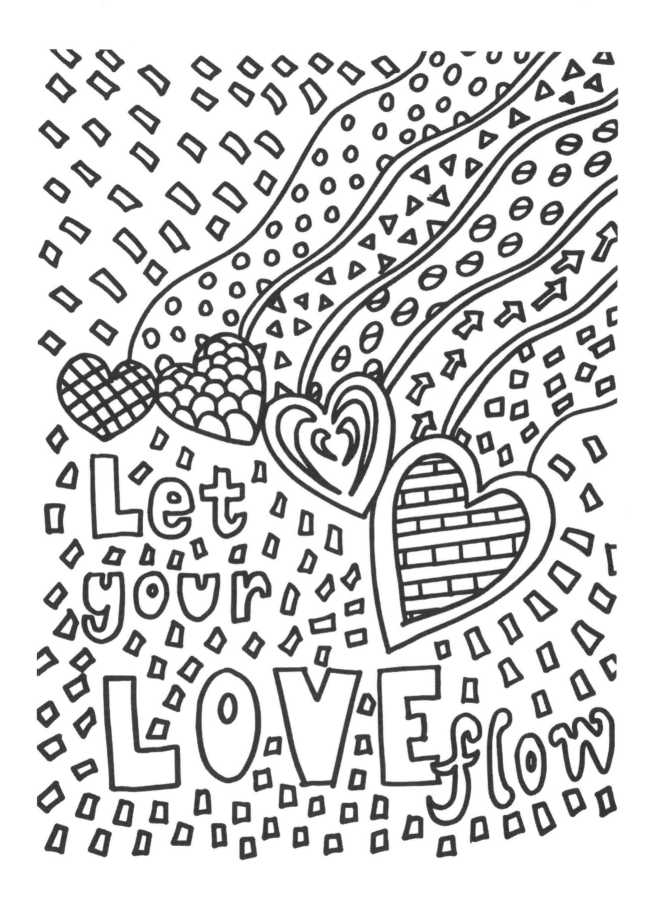

ILLUSTRATED BY: CHRISTINE LI

COLORED BY:

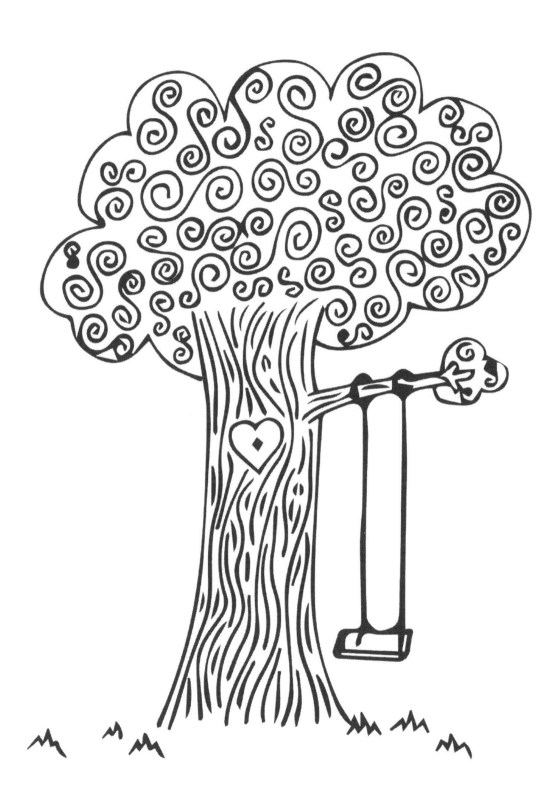

ILLUSTRATED BY: JESSICA LEWER

COLORED BY:

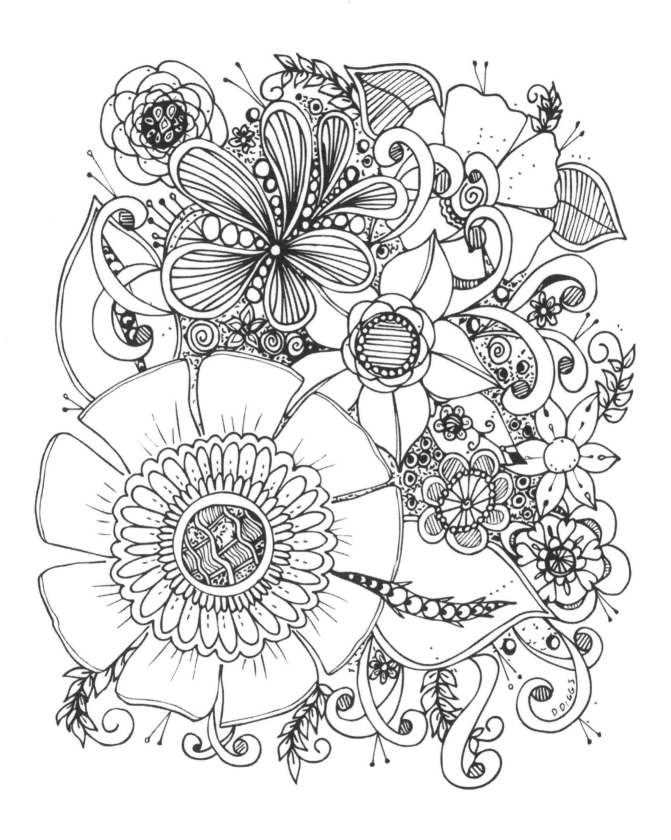

ILLUSTRATED BY: DENISE DIGGS   COLORED BY:

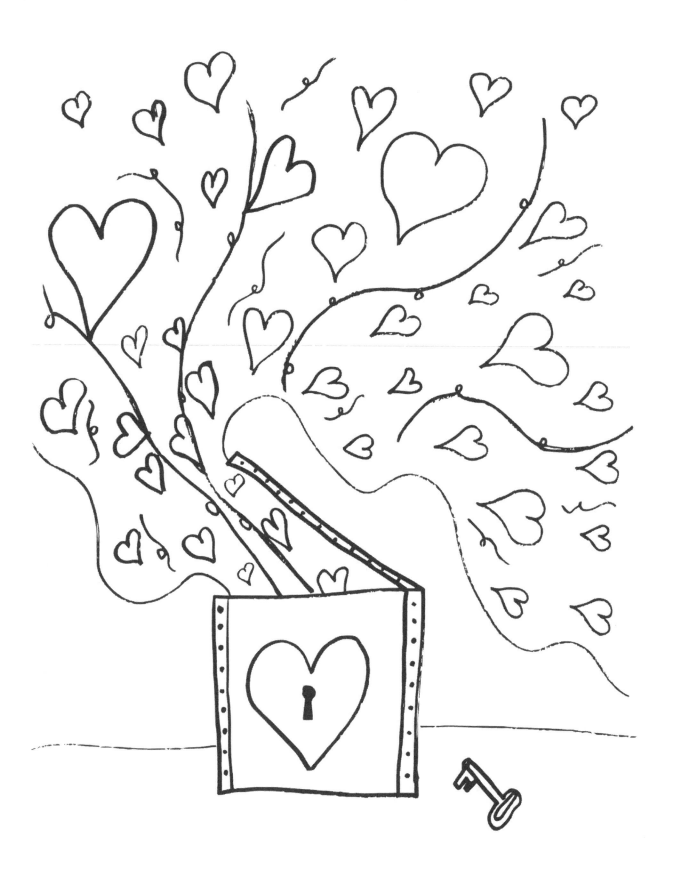

ILLUSTRATED BY: KAY ANDERSON

COLORED BY:

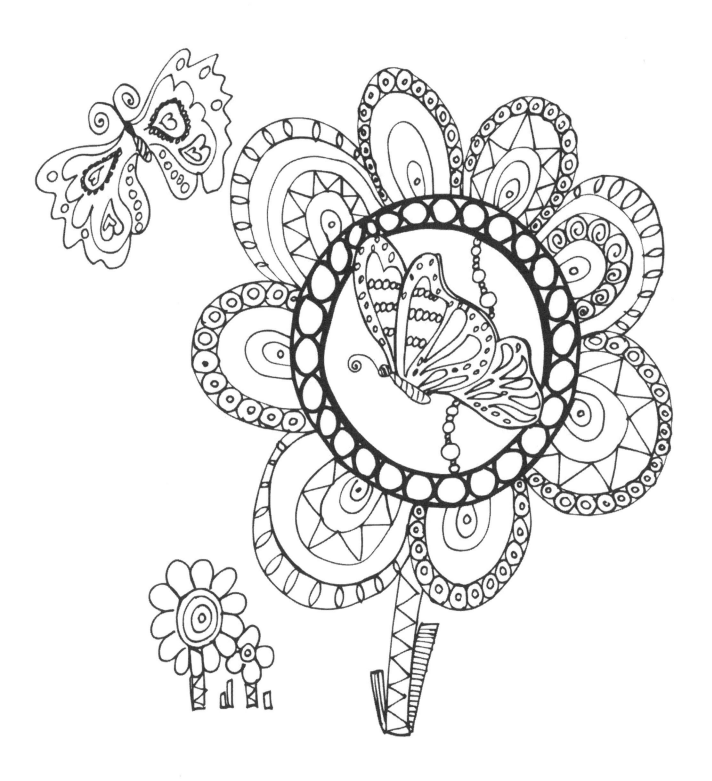

ILLUSTRATED BY: NATALIA GABREA   COLORED BY:

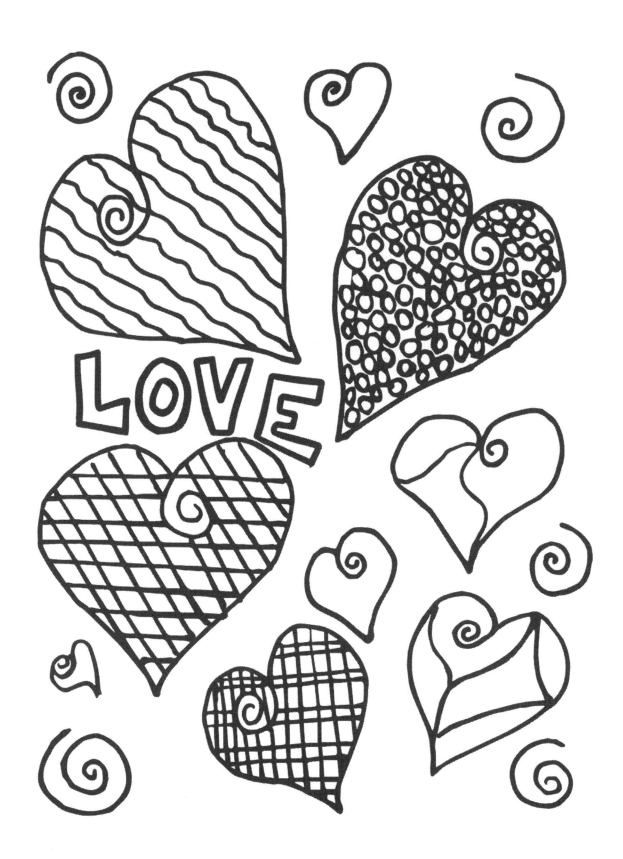

ILLUSTRATED BY: ANN LEACH   COLORED BY:

ILLUSTRATED BY: LINDA RAGATZ   COLORED BY:

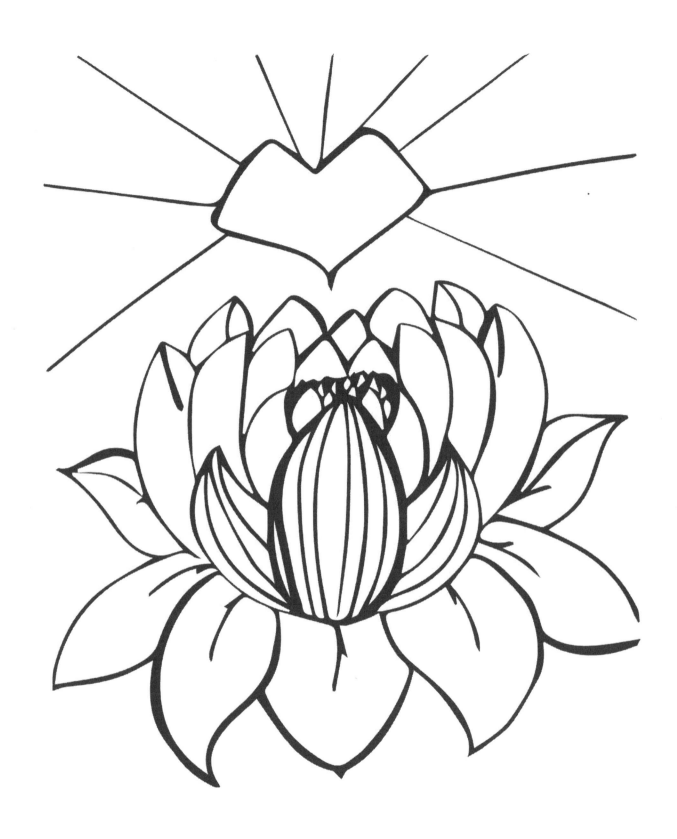

ILLUSTRATED BY: SARAH BATCHELL   COLORED BY:

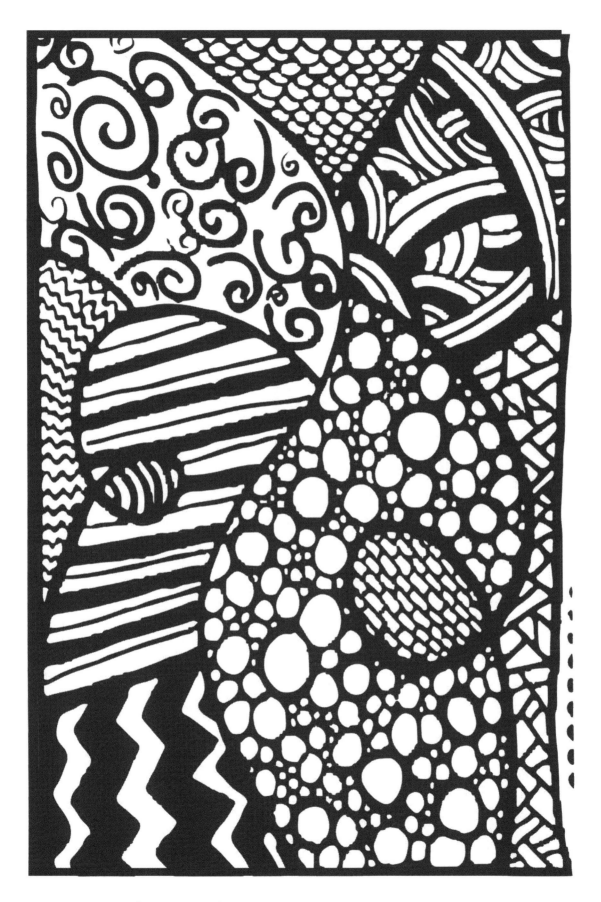

ILLUSTRATED BY: MICHELLE BASTIAN   COLORED BY:

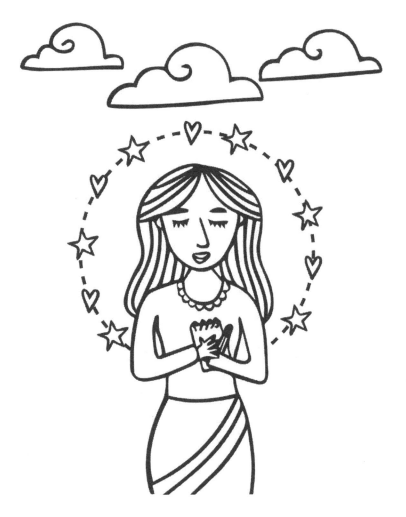

Thank you to everyone who contributed to the making of this book. It was a true collaboration of artists of all ages from around the world.

Please share your final coloring pages online: #DGFBook1

With all my Love,

Diane Bleck

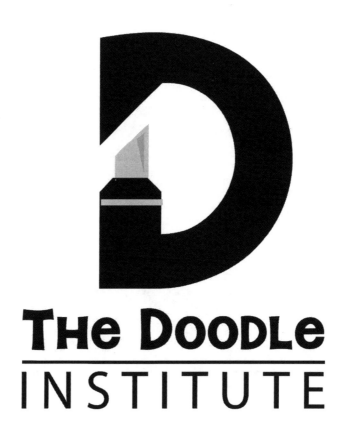

The Doodle
INSTITUTE

Check out our online videos & Courses:
www.doodleinstitute.com

Made in the USA
Columbia, SC
12 April 2018